Aleksandar Ristović (1933–1994) published more than twenty books of poetry in his lifetime, as well as a collection of literary essays. He lived in Belgrade, where he was employed as an editor of children's books and where he received a number of Yugoslavia's major literary prizes.

Charles Simic, who was born in Yugoslavia in 1938 and left in 1953, now lives in the United States. He has had two volumes of poetry published by Faber: *Frightening Toys* (1995) and *Looking for Trouble* (1997). He has been the recipient of numerous awards for his poems and translations, among them the Pulitzer Prize in 1990.

D1566946

ALEKSANDAR RISTOVIĆ

DEVIL'S LUNCH

Selected Poems

*translated from Serbian and introduced
by Charles Simic*

faber and faber

LONDON·NEW YORK

First published in 1999
by Faber and Faber Limited
3 Queen Square London WC1N 3AU
Published in the United States by Faber and Faber, Inc.,
a division of Farrar, Straus and Giroux, Inc., New York

Photoset by Wilmaset Ltd, Wirral
Printed in England by MPG Books Limited,
Victoria Square, Bodmin, Cornwall

All rights reserved
© The Estate of Aleksandar Ristović, 1999
This translation © Charles Simic, 1999

Charles Simic is hereby identified as translator of this work
in accordance with Section 77 of the Copyright, Designs and
Patents Act 1988

*This book is sold subject to the condition that it shall not,
by way of trade or otherwise, be lent, resold, hired out or
otherwise circulated without the publisher's prior consent in
any form of binding or cover other than that in which it is
published and without a similar condition including this
condition being imposed on the subsequent purchaser*

A CIP record for this book
is available from the British Library

ISBN 0–571–20008–7

Some of these poems were previously published in *Some Other
Wine and Light*, poems by Aleksandar Ristorić (The Charioteer
Press, Washington, 1989), and more recently in the following
magazines: *Agni, Descant, Field, London Review of Books,
Meridian, Ohio Review, Times Literary Supplement, Verse.*

2 4 6 8 10 9 7 5 3 1

Contents

Introduction

'I'm the devil playing with mice' – ALEKSANDAR RISTOVIĆ

Once in a long while one comes across a poet who strikes one as being absolutely original. One reads a few poems and is both struck by the oddness of their vision and convinced of their authenticity. I will never look at anything again in quite the same way, one realizes instantly, and that's what happens. From that day on, another pair of eyes has cunningly joined our own.

The poetry of Aleksandar Ristović has had that effect on me. When I first read his poems in Belgrade in 1982 I was astonished. 'Who is this man?' I kept asking, meaning, How did he come to write the way he did? Nobody could tell me. The literati I showed his poems to were as much puzzled as I was. Even though Ristović published many books of poetry and received three major literary prizes, he has continued to be undeservedly neglected in Yugoslavia. Writers and poets are pack animals, and he, so it appears, did not have the usual ovine instincts. He simply did not belong to any literary movement or clique.

Ristović was born in 1933 in Cacak, a fairly large town some hundred miles south of Belgrade. After receiving a degree in literature from the University of Belgrade, he taught for many years Serbian language and literature in secondary schools in his hometown. In more recent years, and until his death in 1994, he worked as an editor of children's books for a large Belgrade publisher. In addition to his seventeen books of poetry, he published a book of dreams, a book of translations of French poetry and books of short essays.

His poetry, of course, tells us more about him. Ristović is as much at home in rural Serbia as Robert Frost is in New England countryside. He knows its people and their ways intimately, and yet his way of writing about that world is very unusual. Reading him, one is not sure whether the events taking place are in the twentieth century or in some earlier times. His poems remind me of medieval woodcuts illustrating proverbs on dangers and delights of the Seven Deadly Sins. What the anonymous artists have in common with Ristović is the love of the grotesque. Men, women, children, animals, devil and God himself – all their identities are in a flux, they can turn into their opposite in a wink of an eye. They are like those mythical beings, part human, part animal. The parts bicker with one another or they raise hell and make merry.

All great poetry is the contemplation of a few essential images. Ristović has his butchers, his pigs, his glass of wine and many other recurring images. They keep nagging him. Images are more demanding than ideas. They are like dreams that we dream again and again. The silence of the image invites a dialogue. The poet is like someone alone in a movie theater complaining about the projectionist, and talking back to the silent film being shown on the screen. In an essay Ristović praises Homer as the ideal poet because he could with equal skill converse with gods and mortals.

There's a lot of violence and suffering in these poems. Evil rules the world. Good is weak, leaving us only with the memory of a few moments of kindness and beauty. Many twentieth-century poets have believed in angels, but Ristović may be the only one who believes in the devil. When we least expect it, some demon is liable to jump out of our mouths. For Ristović we are always tottering between good and evil, matter and spirit, and that he finds pretty funny. 'The sense of the funny is the true sense of the tragic,' Russell Edson says, and that is pretty much Ristović's own view of things.

It is not just in the works of such painters as Vermeer and El Greco that light and shadow are the stage directors of metaphysical mysteries. They may be present in poems too. Such light exists nowhere in nature and what we are seeing in these painters, and in such poets as Ristović, may be the glow of that inward light, the very same one that makes our dreams discernible at night. Otherwise, how are we to explain the paradoxical quality of these poems? They are at the same time clear and enigmatic, full of light and crisscrossed with shadows.

This book is a selection from a huge body of work, much of it of very high quality. Ristović wrote long poems, poetic sequences, autobiographical narratives in verse, short poems and prose poems. His range of subject matter is not vast. He is both single-minded and endlessly inventive. He may give the impression that he is a kind of primitive, but his essays show him to have been a sophisticated reader of literature. He knew American, English and French poets the best. 'It's not the poet who makes the world around him poetic,' Ristović wrote, 'but the world that surrounds him that makes him a poet.' It does so, he said, for the sake of poetry and what it has always strived to do: make the things of the world real as well as our own fleeting presence among them.

Charles Simic

DEVIL'S LUNCH

The glimmer of gold

Nobody reads poetry anymore,
so who the hell are you
I see bent over this book?

Untitled

Time of fools is coming,
time of the fairground tent
and the one with a clown's face
  cursing God.

Time of the peacock quill,
the quill that glides from right to left
over the paper downside up.

Time when you won't lift your little finger
without dipping into something
they call indecent.

Time of fools is coming,
time of the know-nothing professor
and the book that can't be cracked open
  at either edge.

Work for me, the gravedigger and the one
in whose absence I wrote this poem

It's a nice day, Mr Gravedigger.
Rest a little by the open grave
and watch them climb the hill.

They have the same faces
as the one you've readied
    the spacious chamber for.
The same bellies, hands, anklebones,
    and almost the same clothes.

They carry flowers and a long casket
with its lid slightly raised,
under which a narrow hand is visible.

Go on with your work. Don't think
or brag about your vast experience,
which, in any case, always gets muddled
    with unrelated matters.

The law

Put aside your papers, your Honor,
and take note of the one who has entered
   your chamber
the day before the public hearing.

She says she's to bear her brother's child,
in the meantime, deftly concealing
   her swollen belly
with a richly colored cape.

A dog sits before your door,
a dog who belongs to the hapless one
   with holes in her shoes.
It whines and rattles its chain.

Do her the favor she asks of you,
insert a paragraph with a number not to be found
in the book with heavy covers.

She'll exit as she came in, bowing low,
while tucking her tiny hands
in the folds of her woolen cape.

Meditation on the rope

You won't be able to bear my weight, O rope!
You'll break the moment I begin to think
this must be that long-promised eternity
with its one and only blurred object rising before me.

I'd better make use of you for some other purpose:
like holding one end, while the one wearing
a T-shirt and tennis shoes holds the other end
as she tries to pull me across the line in the sand.

I'd better leave out other possibilities
and do what Baudelaire did by picturing
a mischievous couple whose misery does not prevent them
from engaging in bizarre sexual practices.

Be, then, the rope by which they pull the cow through the
    wheat,
and the rope by which they toll the village bell at midnight,
and the rope they tie around the waist while descending
into the well with a bucket in one hand and a lantern in the
    other.

Flirting with a pig

Come to me, you who dress yourself in court finery
    while wallowing in the mud,
come to me with your piggish eyes averted.
I have some understanding for your embarrassment and
    for your vanity.

It's not right for a poet to like the same things you do,
but there's something dear to me in your debauchery
to which you yield with everlasting ambivalence.

Still, the devil waits for you in the slaughterhouse.
He has fat fingers, a sheepskin coat and an assortment
    of fine cutting tools.
He stands in the middle of a large room with legs spread
    apart, wearing rubber boots and playing with knives.

In the meantime, his helper rinses a wooden pail
and watches the boss's daughter climb down the ladder
lifting her skirt so that her pink soles and shins show.

Come to me out of your mire, Madam Pig,
I'd like to whisper sweet nothings into your large ear
    before they lead you away,
by turns throwing curses and praises upon you.

Of time and events

Time, you fancy the one who blows
into a thin straw scattering bubbles
from his childhood terrace.

And the one who descends the stairs
trailed by dogs and female servants,
after pretending for years that he was dead.

And the one who fills his small room
with the squeak of musical instruments
while sitting in a chair with his head thrown back.

And the one with eyeglasses in his lap
who sits with head pressed against the wall
and points to a place known only to himself.

Be kind to me, too, who am not afraid
to be with all of them, together or separately,
and at the same time.

Landscape with snow

What makes your hand so skilled, pig butcher?
The one with a desperate look just a second ago
now gazes at you humbly and even with trust.

Head thrown back, ears cocked, your belle
inspects the morning sun which has the shape of a blade,
while you press her between your knees,
not letting the cigarette go out of your mouth.

What causes your sudden laughter, butcher,
as you stand next to what only a while ago was living,
peeling her skin off as if it were an expensive dress
and sticking your greasy hands deep into her womb?

Truly, what is the reason for your silence
at the table with a white cloth and a blurred glass of wine,
while country fiddles resound throughout the house
and people whisper among themselves about this or that?

You sit in the sled tucked in embroidered covers,
dressed the way a pig butcher is supposed to be dressed,
and stroking the thin neck of a farmer's daughter,
her ears and round arms,
while all around you the snow keeps falling.

Workroom

You who are making a big cape out of mice-skin,
put aside briefly the tools of your trade:
the cushion studded with pins and the narrow scissors.

She isn't paying attention to your sewing,
but keeps squinting, instead, through the steamed window
at the man in a carriage wearing earrings.

Don't poke her with your needle
in her blushing cheek and forehead,
or in her hair arranged in a bun.

Don't frighten her with the story
of a tragic death in a tailor's workroom.
Don't do her a wrong unintentionally.

Go and finish what you've started,
threading a new thread in a new needle,
while recalling other voices in times of winter holidays.

Gingerbread heart

Make me a long coat of heavy cloth, tailor,
the kind that won't fray,
and of a dark color,
so no one will notice the cigarette ashes.

Make the dark trousers of the same material,
to last as long as I want them to,
wearing them to visit many cities, villages,
and other out-of-the-way places.

Make me a dark vest, O tailor,
in which to sit at a banquet table
with a rich man's rose in the buttonhole,
surrounded by happy faces.

Make me a dark jacket, tailor, with wide, deep pockets
to clench my fists in, while watching the one
they're dragging from my table into the bushes,
which after a few moments begin to shake.

Dead leaves

Danton is waiting to die
but the day just won't break.
His vest is full of lice
and he has water in his boots.
On his face there are already signs
of his exceptional destiny.
He watches me from that great distance
walk under the trees
and gather dead leaves
with a long stick ending in a spike.

Despair

You opened the matchbox.
There was a single match left.
You took it out, so now
the box was empty.
You put three ladybugs in it.
With that one match you set
the box on fire,
and while it burned,
giving off just a little smoke,
you turned towards me,
to laugh in my face.

from *Stain on the negative*

Happy is the matron
covered with evening soapsuds.
Christ stands behind her,
barefoot in wooden sandals.
He pours water over her
from a golden pitcher
and hands her a cloth
with dirty pictures on it.

Inconsequential memory

In one of the pre-war restaurants, my mother
is reading a newspaper article about Alice B. Toklas
entertaining a circle of famous friends.

Between the tearoom and the county courthouse,
autumn wind creases the dresses of the few ladies
who climb or descend the wooden steps in no apparent
  order.

Between the high-school playground and the library,
a man on a bicycle transports rolls of film
from one cinema to the other for the 5:30 showing.

My mother powders her face, hides her small wrinkles,
catches the eye of the waiter, beckons to him,
then pays for the ice cream and leaves the paper on the
  table.

At the very same time, a few left-wing students
stand on the corner of Vojvode Stepe and Ovcarska streets
talking about hunger, sexual abstinence and the slitting of
  wrists,

while Alice B. Toklas puts on her riding clothes,
sniffs the scent of lovemaking on her finger,
and calls Gertrude to her aid, suddenly confused by the
  change in her sex and the toy she holds in her hand.

Interrogation in front of devil's signature
and other lessons

Did you drink enough water from the empty glass,
   funny guy?
Did you pour soup into a bottle and try to drink it in one
   swig
(while the one you're trying to make laugh
hid her face and screamed for you to stop)?

Did you ride backwards holding the horse by his tail?
Did you use one of her scarves as a saddle
as you rode off wearing nothing but long socks
(while the one you're trying to make laugh
sat on her doorstep blowing on her spectacles)?

Did you make the suckers part with their money?
Did you invest it in some shady scheme
so that it grew a hundred times
(while the one you're trying to make laugh
stripped down to her finger-wide panties)?

Did you drive a small car through the wheat fields into the
   hills?
Did you park in the churchyard
Under the belfry and the cross
(while the one you're trying to make laugh
was already pulling the bell rope)?

Did you shuffle the papers of those condemned to die
and those to be freed? Did you
enter your devil's signature on some document
of extraordinary importance
(while the one you're trying to make laugh
stood next to you holding the inkwell and pressing down
on the names with the official blotter)?

Maids

One is in the cellar,
the other up in the attic.
One carries a lamp and a platter into a dark room for
  guests sensitive to cold,
the other sits behind the house
staring at the moon rising over the nearby trees.
One travels by village bus forty kilometers through a
  snowstorm,
the other tries to light a fire while sitting on the iron bed
  next to her mother who is already seeing angels, like
  hundreds and hundreds of fireflies.
One weeds the onions, waters the garden, chases a chicken,
the other stands by the window holding before her face a
  rose-colored leaf that gives off no scent.
One is at the table where she diligently polishes dishes,
  knives, spoons, and forks,
while a bee, which has flown through the window, in vain
  seeks a way out, bumping into the curtain and the pane,
the other one smokes strong tobacco
with some punk from the neighborhood, raising and
  lowering her eyes constantly.
But soon the night will be here
and both of them will find themselves in their own beds,
one with a novel on her knees lit by a table lamp,
the other one already dreaming the first dream of the night:
  the seashore, the thin line of waves and herself
  losing articles of her clothing, one by one, while walking

with greater and greater speed toward someone whose
   face
is hidden by a shadow of a nearly phantasmagoric rose.

Old motif

For whom are you intended, wine in that corked bottle
on the white tablecloth,
next those swaying flowers,
while some young girl sweeps the still empty room?

You'll untie the tongue of the silent one,
turn the fool into a wise man,
and to the weakling you'll give courage
to act out on his secret desire.

Out of the wise man you'll make a fool
who squanders his riches in the company of spoiled
    servants and flunkies,
and who promises to the buxom cashier
a woodland cottage with pine needles on the floor.

Perhaps you'll spin the head of a beautiful woman,
so she quits the table for one of the upstairs rooms
dogged by some worthless fellow
who makes up verses with only one purpose in mind?

Briefly, perhaps, you'll change the old man
into that youth in the tavern who sings and taps his foot
all the time making frequent visits to the lavatory
to flirt with the one counting small coins in a cigar box.

For whom are you intended, wine in the corked bottle?
Through whose veins will you send your merry little flame,
making him behold the most ordinary things
in many strange and unaccustomed ways?

To a fool

What you know, O fool,
no one else does.
And what no one else knows,
I can't touch.

Truly, what is it you've got in your head
while you shuck corn in a wooden bowl
or poke a bug in the direction of a girl's arm?

The key has turned twice in the lock.
The menu of erotic services lies open on the table
next to the soup, a pair of sheer stockings and a rose.

Lazybones, you're too much!
Between Something and Nothing you chose what in truth is
    Nothing:
gabbing under the bedcovers or leaving one's own breath
    on the round windowpane.

These fellows, who come running in city clothes,
    wearing badges, will take you under the arms
and drag you into the meadow,
where her body twists and turns in various seductive poses.

About hope and dissipation

O where haven't I and when didn't I do it!

In the rustic privy with the breeze cooling me
through the cracks between the boards,
in the toilet of the village priest under the lit porcelain lamp,
in the school lavatory with the notebook held
between my teeth and my face turning red,
in a rich lady's bathroom
smelling of angels and Christmas trees
as she watches me through a two-way mirror
and slowly paints her lips red,
in our family bathroom with its hand towel
and toilet paper covered with messages,
intended for the next user,
who arrives out of breath,
paying no attention to the printed words.

O where haven't I and when didn't I do it!

On my way to someplace else,
watching mice on a moonlit night
move their residence from one crapper to another,
in the toilet of the Creator Himself,
who beforehand slips me the key
and discreetly reminds me of other obligations
while activating a concealed microphone
to record all articulate and inarticulate sounds
and simultaneously broadcast them

to a gathering of eminent scientists
engrossed in distinguishing, in that hubbub,
sighs, bells, a hen cackling,
and someone's timorous confession
of hope and dissipation.

Privy

Through a crack on the right
you can see the red rooster,
and through the one on the left,
with a bit of effort,
you can see the table,
the white cloth
and a bottle of wine.
Behind your back, if you turn,
you'll make out the sheep
trying to fly with their woollen wings.
And through the heart-shaped
hole in the door,
someone's cheerful face
watching you shit.

Monastic privy

In the back of the nunnery
there's a small privy
with a half-open door and evening visitors.
While one is inside,
another waits her turn
with her nose in the book.
And while the first one exits,
straightening her robes,
her face almost radiant,
the other one steps in,
peeks into the spotless hole,
trembling with terror,
that what lies at the bottom
may leap into her face
and leave a mark on her flushed cheek
in the shape of a devil's cross.

Lavatory theater

The hero strides on stage,
unbuttons his old-fashioned trousers
and lets them slide to his feet
where they lie in neat folds.
He sits on the toilet facing the public,
while in the next stall,
reserved for ladies,
the one who plays the role of Phaedra
goes about the same business.
With her back to the audience,
she lifts her skirt all of a sudden
and shows off her gorgeous ass.
What follows are sounds
that make the faces of those
sitting in the boxes, not to mention
those in the first few rows,
turn cherry-red.

Discreet lavatory

This the lavatory you enter
almost on tiptoe
after having been made to change
into soft slippers,
your hat and business card
left with the fat lady attendant
who follows you with a look
of maternal understanding
right up to the potty,
and then waits for you at the exit,
her voice tinged with melancholy
as you hang your head in shame
dutifully entering your name
in the restroom's book of visitors.

Lavatory library

The shelves of dark wood
are lined with works of classic authors.
The light falls
over the reader's shoulder
onto the open book
while he roosts comfortably
on the seat with a round opening,
exerting himself only to solve
the mystery of the obstacle
that lies between him
and the true meaning of the text,
in this library famous for
its missing pages, implying
readers in a hurry, for whom
Dante's or Homer's verses
and the writings of some scribbling nobody
have equal value.

The drunk's lavatory

The drunk's lavatory is no different
from that of a stray dog.
There it is, suddenly taking the shape
of an abandoned house, stone steps,
a garden with September roses,
a lone tree, a graveyard cross,
or some museum whose naked statues
can be seen through one of its windows.
In the last resort, a shed in the yard
where tools and work-clothes are kept,
and which he enters in desperate need,
fumbling with the belt and buttons
of his trousers made heavy by the pint
sticking out of his back pocket.

Out in the open

While crossing a field,
someone who at that moment
is preoccupied with thoughts of suicide
is forced by nature's call
to delay the act,
and so from his squatting position
finds himself taking pleasure
in some blades of grass,
as if seeing them for the first time
from that close,
while his cheeks redden,
and he struggles to pull from his pocket
a piece of paper
with its already composed
farewell note.

Centaur with face lit up on both sides

Don't singe the curl on my beard, O barber
    of the ratty old barbershop!
Let my face ignite into hundreds of fiery ringlets,
and let each one be snuffed out before I rise
    from your chair with its cleverly adjustable backrest.

Don't sneak up on me with long scissors
    in a hand smelling of rich perfume,
to snip around my ears and the back of my head
    with a few quick turns.
I want to leave just as I came in: with one hand scratching
    my head, and the other stuck in my belt.

Don't whisper in my ears words that make me blush
    (if only I could divine their meaning).
Don't take me by the arm, leaning into my face,
to one of the back rooms where young men kiss
    on the lips and try on evening gowns.

We don't speak the same language, Mr Barber
    of the ratty old barbershop!
You've misunderstood my appearance and my manner
while I try to make you see what every child knows
    as he plays with substitute toys.

Devil's lunch

A thorn is enough for him.
An apple made of iron.
The nipple of a girl who paces her home
wearing only a cotton slip.
An ear of a pig is enough.
The bug crawling between two empty dishes.
The child puffing into a dandelion.
The withered limbs of an old woman
on her deathbed.
The limbs of a young woman
waiting for her lover
with one hand on her breast
and the other on her lips.

What he eats for lunch
he vomits for dinner
into a rose bush,
or under a Christmas tree.

A road meant to be walked

Where are you taking me, road meant to be walked
which I tramp keeping to the middle,
protected by a hooded cape and shoes with thick soles?

You don't get shorter, but only lengthen,
since the distance I have already covered is added to
    what still lies ahead of me,
and the time I wasted is multiplied by the time I'm going to
    waste.

From time to time you plunge downwards, as if gone mad,
or you climb light-footed up a hill, not holding to anything,
while water drips drop by drop out of a bowl into someone's
    red mouth.

Where are you taking me, road meant to be walked
as the rain slackens my swaying arms at the same time
    it lashes my back to make me hurry
and frogs no bigger than a child's hand leap out of the grass
    before me?

Happiness

The mouse is golden
and so are the turtle and the spider,
and even the centipede,
and the pebble with which you try
to get rid of it
without leaving your bench,
from which one can view many other
things and golden beings.

Regarding walking on water

I'm trying to walk on water,
and you know, at times,
somehow, I manage to do so.

Believe me, the trick is
to fix on something else
besides one's own gravity.

And so, here I am
teaching others to walk on water.
They wet the bottom of their trousers, but they learn.

Thus, when a few of us find ourselves
    walking on water,
we lean into one another's faces
and scream with excitement.

My wife also walks on water;
sometimes all alone.
She carries a small apple in her hands
    and doesn't make a peep.

Black on white or green background

My crow prefers walking to flying,
be it over a green or a snowy field.
Perhaps he's come to the conclusion
it's more dignified to walk than to fly?

At times, we meet alone in a field.
He won't step aside and neither will I.
We stand facing each other:
one stubborn creature opposite another.

Then, one of us gives up,
let's say he does – but he doesn't fly off,
he merely turns and steps
to the left, or to the right.

I'm thinking, this crow of mine is not a bird.
He just looks like one
with his beak, wings and claws,
while his intentions and manner are human.

Now, as I watch from my window at dusk
the snow whirl around the bald trees,
I hear him cawing to himself,
clearly unwilling to hold back what's on his mind.

Some woman is throwing at his feet
trinkets, cheap jewelry and pearls.
Finally, she bares her plump breast for him,
and the crow lets out a sigh.

House spider

This spider waits for Sunday,
goes from one end of his web
    to the other,
small but conspicuous like a smudge
    on a sunlit face.

At rest, he fixes his gaze at the wall
over which flit the shadows of creatures
grown immortal in their idleness.

His web is like my tobacco pouch.
The philosophy he draws from it
shirks neither suffering nor pleasure.

Every trespasser is an easy mark.
Witty, quick as a flame, he makes them
    pay their debts,
occasionally even giving back small change.

In a room with table-lamps and an antique chandelier
sits the poet, Sergei Yesenin,
making the lady of the house titter
by reciting funny verses to her.
She wears a fine sealskin coat,
while he is shoeless in red woolen socks.
Large soft snowflakes are falling outdoors.
Yesenin has the face of a child.
His cheeks are flushed with wine,
which every so often he swills
from the green jug under the table.
In the street, the revolutionaries
are in the midst of their grim business.
They are shooting the bourgeoisie,
and along with them, of course,
the bogus revolutionaries.

Small lamp

Small lamp,
light up my face
from time to time.
Don't pretend
you don't see me.

I'm here
wherever that is,
still
doubled over
my worries.

History

I died in 1864. I was a child with a head of lead and lips to which snow stuck. My father trailed after me trying to get my attention with gestures that would make anyone catch his breath. For a few more years, he sold attar of roses, lanterns for guides and silk caps. I watched him from inside my coffin one snowy evening when the scent of the elder tree was in the air.

Strange students

The buzzing in the next room
must come from tiny insects
who recently took up residence there.
For the time being, they're invisible.

In the evening, as I listen to them,
I have the impression that they're memorizing
in concert a particular subject,
most likely something to do with botany.

Once in a while, they come to a sudden stop,
as if to hear their teacher speak:
his strictness, that they find so frightening,
cloaked in silence.

When they resume, it's on a higher note,
as if now competing with each other.
I'm beginning to recognize certain groupings
and among them, one or two gifted individuals.

And, of course, a few real dummies, too.

Mythology

Lead the horse out of the pasture,
examine his teeth, nostrils, left and right eye.
Run your hand over his sweaty flanks
and over his mane. Lean your forehead
on his. Speak to him in a low voice
as if to a woman from whom you expect a lot.
Look at his worn horseshoes.
Be careful as you approach from the rear
to measure the length of his tail
and bend over to scoop his droppings
with a wooden shovel and a broom of twigs.
Take the horse to the one who's been watching you,
all this time, whip in hand,
chain-smoking in jodhpurs and leather boots
on whose high polish you can see your weary face.

Metamorphosis

I held in the palm of my hand
her royal highness, the frog,
and felt her belly swell up,
the tendons of her legs tighten
as she readied herself to jump.
The water lay green in the stone well
while the frog watched me with her red eyes
out of that other world
from which her cold blood
and her wet skin come,
and perhaps her ability
to transform herself many times
without losing anything
of what she started with.

She jumped, as if I had released a spring,
leaving behind, briefly,
the memory of her weight,
her beggary and her riches.

Comparison

They say, Ulysses did not love the sea,
and that's why he was the captive
of sea breezes, sea storms and waves
that are like bedspreads trimmed with lace.
The same is true of me. Not loving poetry
and still yielding to it, I have become its captive
and can offer the reader nothing but myself.
Like the one who continuously switches
from oars to sail and back, gambling everything
on a story in which he will not be recognized
among the carefully picked images:

I'm that pig.
I'm that strawberry in the garden.
I'm that pipe smoke.
I'm that foam at the mouth.
I'm that wheel.
I'm that hand the wheel passes over
as it moves crushing gravel
parallel to another wheel.

The touch of absence

Nothing exists, except a small object,
something formless that can only
loosely be called an object:
without hardness, color or movement,
without width or length,
or any other verifiable sign of its presence.
It exists merely in our touching hope
that we'll see it and use it,
or be of some use to it,
do with it what the hand does with keys,
flashlight, pliers,
or my always open book, for instance.

Tree

How antiquated a tree is! How old-timey,
its inclination to rustle in the evening
while I walk home from the library with books under my
    arms.
Its branches sway the way the wind wants them to
and its beauty lies in what a man or child
bears in his heart as he runs under it.
Perhaps only Plato expected to find wisdom
in such constant motion. First one, and then another
branch, fails to inscribe a circle,
merely arousing in us certain associations
at which we arrive by swapping our experience
of the real for our experience of the imaginary.
And how old-fashioned I am, who loves to dawdle
under a tree and seek in its appearance
some symbol of mortality and eternal life.

Someone else

Suppose you stand behind someone who has just turned
     his back on you
and imagine that he is you, while someone else stands
behind you seeing what you see?

If it happens to be a woman (and why not?),
and you are that woman with all her knockout looks
you are also watching from the back?

If there are two of them, a man and a woman,
then you are both. You have in equal measure
the attributes of one as well as of the other.

Only if it is you imagining that you are seeing yourself
     from the back,
then you are not who you are.
There's nothing in common between you and that
     unlucky fellow.

Daydreaming in the midst of spring labors

Don't touch these flowers! Not you who are here,
but you who are over there. Like them,
you are a brainchild of my memory and my hope.
Let the devil himself help you come to me
growing smaller and smaller. I don't care
about the flowers, which I merely invented
to give myself another reason to address you.
The new day throws torn bits of an important paper
into our faces. On the table, there's bread
made out of soot, soup out of rust and,
as you'd expect, wax-cakes. I accept
the offer you made to me in dreams.
I eat your hands and breasts every evening,
I slowly chew your fingers and toes
and your eyes with their meaningful look.

This is your bed, your rose, your moonlight
on the coverlet and at the edge of the pillow.
We dreamed of the same day which we now recount
to each other, bringing up overlooked details.
I touch your corporeal being, exalting you
with my own insignificance and my incomparable
images of you. Nothing and nothing
pay us a visit accompanied by another nothing.
As is the custom, they're incorporeal.
One of them speaks of beloved poets giving us

a reason to disappear forever by turning warily
into a potato, lovely primrose, beet and an onion.

I'm smaller than a poppy seed while I gaze at you,
lit by many colored rays of light and your own
love of yourself. I mention north wind, heavy wine,
the builder ghost and the ghosts who tear down
the cosmos, using words of the poets and wrenches
and pliers made out of our own flesh and bone.

Some enter the tavern, the others exit

Some enter the tavern, the others exit.
There's a dish of violets and a lit lamp
on the table and someone's two legs
in sheer stockings under it.

A woman leans her face into mine.
The lamb is also in the tavern, but we don't call it that.
Now we can even smell the flowers
at the next table, not just on our own.

The one who held the book dropped it.
There's a blue flame on the spot where the book fell.
The young waiter carries small saucers
with frogs in them who are ready to jump.

My mother climbs down a high ladder.
Her fingers are frozen and her cheeks and mouth
are almost white. One can hear two people talking
without seeing either of them.

I'm a small boy studying English in a room lit
by a russet light. A small woman, whose breasts are
like two eggs, is helping me. Someone whose name
is Dylan Thomas has joined our game of student and
    teacher.

We call to each other in muffled voices.
Soon we'll die the same death, only in different places:
I, in a small library where books lie in disorder on the
    shelves,
you, in some room where persons of different sexes
    hide their faces from each other.

from *Skin and bones*

The priest and the mourners
are climbing a hill,
the dead man lies smiling
in the coffin of yellow wood.

The red-faced priest reads
from a black prayer-book
while stealing peeks
at the young woman next to him.

His prayer has brought
tears to her eyes,
she imagines his hand
between her breasts.

Even the deceased
has propped himself on an elbow.
The spring rain
beats on his chest and face

as he listens closely
to what the priest is saying.
Finally, he shrugs his shoulders
and lies back down.

from *Canvas*

Long-legged bridegroom,
long-legged bride
swinging from the roof-beam.

❧

The teacher sits under a white tree
reading from a white book.
A flock of white doves all round him.

❧

Crazy house
full of batty girls,
the guests have already stripped
down to their underwear.

❧

The pig is squirming
in the bathtub,
his master is tickling him
with a long knife.

❧

Next to the bed,
army boots and a pair of high heels.
The rest you don't see.

❧

She stepped on a turd,
took off her shoe.
O grass, is that your job too?

&

A perfect kind of day
for accusations and arrests
on the street or at home.

&

The doctor is with the dying man.
He is helping him urinate
in a pot decorated with dirty pictures.

&

The boy sent to the principal's office
hesitates at the door.
Inside he hears the cries of love.

&

The prioress is naked
in the wooden tub.
Next to it, a pig and a black rooster.

&

The lovers of poetry
sit in the first rows,
suitably attired
and with a special expression
on their faces.

❧

A sparrow flew into a well.
In the water
children's faces are reflected.

❧

The leaves are at our heels.
We are running
from the leaves.

The gathering of the metaphysicians

Some speak of the supreme,
of the final throw of dice,
of what is *nothing* to some and nothing to others,
of images, just before we drift off into dreams,
of rose compared to green and rose next to green,
of afternoons gathering seashells on a pebbly beach,
of the nonexistence of one and the nonexistence of the other,
of the metaphysics of objects and the metaphysics of time in
    which this and that object came into being,
of memories, of course,
of sacrilege,
of the confession of some woman leaning toward your face,
of death which leaves partial evidence here and there not
    allowing us to see it in its totality,
of Nothing, which alone can be proven and cannot be
    refuted,
of the transcendental (being unable to distinguish one's own
    voice from thunder and the noise of objects),
of me speaking of any old thing, beginning with the lowest
    and proceeding to the highest:
of the misery of a man in a village outhouse watching the
    oats and the rye fields sway,
of the misery of some other man in his own bed or in the
    bed of his neighbor,
of a hen,
a tripod,

hardness and softness,
and the shiftiness of disciples and the steadfastness of
    masters.

The essential

I was not allowed to live my life,
so I pretended to be dead
and interested solely in things
a dead man could be interested in:
petrified reptiles,
museum bric-à-brac,
fake evidence passed off as truth.
I felt a great need to be really dead,
and so at all times I wore
a mask made of wood
on which someone occasionally drew,
with colored pencils,
the look of contentment,
impatience, desire, bliss,
or the look of someone who is thinking
about an entirely different matter.

The graves of poets

My wife is reading a book of great poets.
While we lie tucked in bed under the same lamp,
I imagine their graves in various places:
the grave of Walt Whitman
with branches, flowers, leaves,
the American flag and empty beer cans
left by a party of young people.

At Pushkin's grave, my melancholy summons
the images from the books I've read,
so, of course, there are birch trees and deep snow
all the way up to his resting place.
The tomb of T. S. Eliot, cut severely
out of stone and marble, has a young woman
hanging around at all hours,
uncomprehending and a bit daffy.

Other graves of beloved poets I see too,
listening to the verses she reads aloud
in a voice that is, at times, elevated,
at times matter-of-fact, while just then
someone trying to enter the house
fumbles for the key, talking to herself,
scolding her alter ego with a heavy tongue,
three sheets to the wind.

The farmers' market

On the table, there is a glass of water,
the *Education Review*
and one red apple.

On the bed in the corner of the room,
the teacher Drinka is dying
and laughing while dying.

In her mind she is at the farmers' market,
surrounded by naked country people.
They jeer and throw potatoes at one another.

One has hair growing in the palm of his hand,
another has crossed his eyes so far
he can't bring them back where they belong.

Drinka stands among them, scantily dressed,
but whenever someone passes by
and turns to greet her, they grow serious.

Her mouth is stretched from ear to ear,
her white belly is shaking,
and she has made two tight fists.

And that's how she died, laughing –
in fact, she didn't even know
she had died.

They told her that afterwards.

Future-past journey

My grandmother and I are traveling to a monastery
in a rustic coach pulled by a white horse.
Grandma is still a girl, and I am 59 years old.

In her lap, grandma has a basket of lilies-of-the-valley,
and I have a coin in my pocket with which one of
   Christ's tormentors was bribed.
(Soon I'll die, but that's not the subject of this poem.)

The journey takes us from tavern to tavern and soon
we are so tipsy we can barely see each other.
The coachman spies on us and crosses himself secretly.

On the way to our destination, we take into the coach
a beggar who is feebleminded.
He plays a mouth organ and asks nothing in return.

My grandmother and I are traveling to a monastery
between green trees with the air smelling of her lilies
and of the rain beating against our faces.

Go and finally climb that spiral staircase

Go and finally climb that spiral staircase,
carrying your shoes in one hand,
and a church candle in the other.

I'm telling you there's no one upstairs
except an owl above the cracked door.
It won't stir, even as you bring the candle closer.

Don't be startled by the unexpected scent
of lilacs in the misty room. In vain
you'll rummage around trying to find them.

Keep that childlike smile on your face.
It hides everything you really feel:
fear, curiosity and confusion, of course.

Wait a little longer by the cracked mirror,
with the schoolbooks and toys whose owners are
long dead grandfathers and grandmothers.

Owls

Small owls are flying through the dark air
between the winter and the summer house.
Their wings can be heard and also their voices
    as they talk back and forth.

You're playing with a strange object
that sputters fire as you raise it to your face.
You're almost beautiful in that dress
    of silk and sparks.

The small owls continue to flit by
and I imagine tiny women dressed in black
who have suddenly grown wings.

At last, I place my hand in your lap
thinking how natural this is,
and so are the other things
    I want very much to do next.

Now, we are walking under the big trees
in whose high branches the owls sit brooding.
God whispers coarse words into their ears,
    but they stay as they are.

Time and unacceptable human destiny

I see small coaches passing between the trees.
I try to catch them with one hand,
but they continually slip away
to the sound of young women giggling
from the pleasure they take in riding about.

Partridges fly out of the grass, but it's some other
century, some other grass, and the partridges
are not always partridges, but some other bird,
and at times they are even animals.

I see the flowers you've strewn on the floor for my sake.
I see the glass where the drink that was warm yesterday
is now cooling. I find myself before somebody
else's door, where I reach for the bell or call out a name.

In fact, I'm that young man with thick spectacles
    in the library.
I flirt with a lady who wears them too and has
an interest in creative writing. She's all in white
and her smile reveals a row of white teeth
over which she has stuck cellophane like a child.

I see the house where we'll spend our remaining years:
our faces redden in the evening by the small fire
in the big stove. The horses, too, are inside the house
and their presence is truly necessary,
for we have many plans and they include the horses.

There's also a woman who does not know me,
who pretends she doesn't see me,
although I see her huge breasts which have the ability
to speak, as do her feet, stamping the beat
for a certain music lover.

I see the shadows of friends, angelic or devilish.
Some are already dead and know how to converse
with the dead. The others stand in the road pointing
at the Lord and his son,
who imitates everything his father does.

The north wind blows the snow under the door –
and we like that. There's plenty of snow outside,
but the little inside the house is a magic presence.
We won't sweep it till morning, even if the door
refuses to open after many tries.

I see an old man in place of me: he sits
on the doorstep wielding a pencil
while composing verses of uneven quality.
The pages, covered with writing, lie scattered
around the shoes he has taken off
and his almost transparent feet.

Soon, I'll call him into the house,
where they're ladling bean soup this evening
and where they can barely speak with mouths full,
so they use their hands and are fitfully understood
by those who do not, making them smile
at the housewife who uses my poems for a dish rag.

Evening poem

Small candle, illuminating,
not only the saucer you're attached to,
but also the remains of a dinner
and the surrounding objects.

You make the spoons and forks glow,
and also the paper on which
I quickly write these words,
cheered by your presence.

In your weak light, the more distant objects
are endowed with some of the mystery
you yourself contain and reveal
each and every time you are lit.

The keys, for instance, and articles of clothing
thrown over the back of a chair,
a woman's stockings,
bra and woolen dress.

I won't let you go out, small candle.
I attribute to you feminine ways,
a little of a woman's slyness
and some of her mockery.

Of course, I also give philosophical weight
    to your light:
which tells me that the small is to be found
    in the great,
and the great can shrink in size
at the whim of its secretive owner.

Evening with devil's icon and pigs

In the smoke of the living-room's oil lamp,
The family sits at the wooden table wearing only socks.
In a low voice, with eyes closed, someone reads
a newspaper from another century.

True angels turn the pages of thin books.
Some are naked, some wear transparent shirts
through which the moonlight falls
as it does now on my table and my hand as it writes.

Bats hang from the ceiling.
Before they fly, they squeak as if pricked by a pin.
The old bed rocks with the newlyweds.

Someone combs his hair over the hot stove.
The fallen lice crackle.
Then he goes away and we laugh like mad.

Across the living-room, my mother
leads a young man whom she calls the Virgin Jesus.
He struggles to free his hand.
Finally, here he is sitting among us
next to the bread and the wine.

From the pigsty in the yard,
we can hear the pigs having nightmares:
Grandpa is chasing them with a knife,
Some he catches and slits their throats,
the others pass out in fear.

Now there they are all in the dark cellar
between the wine barrels
under the icon which has a devil chuckling
where one of the holy saints ought to be.

I hope you won't give up

I hope you won't give up doing
what you've set out to do,
the same old way, from day to day,
for ever and ever, busy bees.

and you others who, with wondrous
motion of your wings, ventilate
the narrow entrance to your hives,
while nightmarish humming continues inside.

And you horses, pulling wagons loaded with
beer barrels and vegetables
in the summer dusk, while men sit
   in restaurant windows
fanning themselves with leafy twigs.

I hope, too, I will not give up doing
   what I'm always doing,
bent over a scrap of paper with a pencil
   in my hand,
perfectionist, as if engaged in something
   of vast importance,
and greatly pleased with myself.

I'm crazy mother and can hardly stand it

At five in the morning, over the monastery
white, blue and black doves fly.
The prioress sits on a tripod; plants onions in the garden.
A neighbor's boy hurries to the house
high up on the slope of the hill.

Naked to the waist, the nuns examine their breasts
in a small mirror and show beauty marks
and mysterious imprints to each other.
Indeed, the monastery is made of silk,
its doors and windows are silken.
One can hear the flowers weep in pots painted green.

I have drawing material and wooden scissors.
I'm trying to draw a portrait of a woman
in a room full of bats. She has two faces,
two pairs of ears, two noses and a single eyebrow.
As I work, I talk amorously to her while contriving
to erase the smudges from her breasts and thighs.

Every now and then, I can hear the monastery bells
and it's like breathing in the scent of violets.
The one being honored eats honey cakes in the kitchen.
The one in an old-fashioned suit undresses
down to his shirt and shorts,
the floor squeaks from his steps,
the insects in the wax-paper box are swarming.

How do you serve the Lord, women dressed in dark
robes whose faces blush at the very thought of God?
Your fingers are touching your nostrils, your eyebrows
are twisted, your ears, of course, are pricked.
Between the servants' quarters and rooms with stairs
painted red, a hurried glass of wine is welcome.

Put the rose back among the thorns,
that's where the rose belongs and your right hand.
Let the dead rat with swollen belly and stiff legs
be your witness. Walk out of the monastery
with your drawings of young nuns dreaming.
There's an obligatory winter scene and a summer one.
The snow is falling, the caterpillar crawling.

The prioress types a poem about beer and evil omens.
Under the table one of her feet is bare,
on the other one she wears a striped sock.
The very thought of drinking makes her tipsy.
Whenever she bends over the table,
toads hop out of her bosom as real as her verses.

The snow is falling on the balcony where I sit
sipping wine out of a coffee cup, watching the trees.
Various ghosts, drunk and dressed in soldier's uniforms,
draw near me. I can almost touch the one whose name
I cannot remember, no matter how much I try,
while a girl with green curls plays on the harmonica
the song about a bricklayer and the house servant.

Like someone else's breath in your face

How many times will you rise from the table,
gather the dishes,
clean the plates,
how many times will you bend down
to pick up something that fell out of your pocket
while you fumbled for your handkerchief,
how many times will you return to your childhood
by placing a rose in a certain place,
how many times will you
unbutton and button yourself
and go and lie down next to the one
who has a small watch on her wrist
no bigger than a gold bug
at which she glances over your shoulder,
out of long habit
holding her breath
full of tenderness?
How many times will you do this or that,
without being aware
of the time passing,
or the time that still remains to you?

The martyrs

St John hands St Nicholas a small can in which are squeezed, one next to the other, soaked in oil and salt, several headless fish of which neither saint knows where they come from, what river or sea?

St Nicholas opens the can using a small opener with a cross stamped on it to indicate its ownership and with his knife arranges the fish on a plate made of rosewood, blackened and reddened, with a few barely visible cracks here and there.

St John is barefoot and so is St Nicholas. The two of them now bend over a plate while the sun shines and the clouds, with greater urgency than on most days, cut across the sky.

At last the plate is empty, the few drops of grease are sopped up with the remaining morsels of bread, the plate is even washed in the nearby stream and dried in the breeze, while in the distance at the sound of the artillery, houses burn, big chunks of human meat fly, the devil himself slits bellies, punches open women's mouths, devours children and gives everything he does an obscure meaning.

Purgatory

We never even felt our share of the eternal
in what was our life: the moments
from which these bursts of activity
and lethargy are made up,
the similarity between here and there
in inner and outer space. We exchanged life
for its semblance, the object for its shadow,
the visible coin for the invisible riches
whose origins are unknown and whose value
is ambiguous: the body for a wee spirit,
the residue of this creation out of nothing,
as in a diaphanous box. Drop by drop
the borders are in motion, purgatory is open
for those of us holding a carving knife,
a rope, and a hoop made of wood.

In the beginning, there was nothing.
They talked of other things.
Beauty and ugliness were not differentiated
nor did the four elements have the form
we now thrill to wreck our brains over.
In the beginning, there was nothing.
Light and darkness
were just something one imagined.
The water hesitated between two states:
solid and gaseous.
Form was the extension of content
and vice versa.
Man rolled over from his back to his belly
burning sticks
or listening to the waves approach.
In the beginning, there was nothing:
neither a tree
nor a flash of lightning in its branches,
nor death,
nor space that could mean more than itself,
nor a grain of pity,
nor time that could hold in its one hand
both what is real and what is imagined.

Guesswork

I'll die. I won't die.

No, I won't die,
though I see angels,
so close,
I can touch them
with my forefinger,
only
their faces are rubbed out
as if with a child's school eraser.

I'll die. I won't die.

While reading Homer

The first snow has fallen
and I'm reading Homer.
Outside an unknown woman,
dressed in dark colors,
reaches down for a shiny
object in the snow.
It's a gold coin. Of course,
in the windows across the street
I can see heroes,
maidens and gods.
The snow makes them happy,
and so do other,
suchlike, childish thrills.

The return of the warriors

In bitter winter weather, our warriors
have returned from the battle.

They blow on their fingers,
or what's left of their fingers.

They brought back the lamb
they took along with them,

but the lamb no longer bleats
or looks for its mother.

It has other habits now,
so it's hard to call it a lamb still.

During the day, it whines like a dog,
at night, it howls like a wolf.

Everybody runs from it, except the soldiers
who stand around making fun of it.

Small monster

A small monster
brushed me
with its wing,
whacked me
with its tail,
stuck its chickenlike claw
into my eye,
and now wants to
do more to me
with its voice:
its whimpers
and its cries.

About death and other things

How strange will be my death, of which I've been thinking
    since childhood.
A sedentary old man leaving a small-town library
leans to one side and gradually collapses on the lawn.

I've every reason to believe that I'll experience
what the others have experienced
while I climb the stairs carrying my supper in a plastic bag,
not even turning to look at the one coming down,
curly-haired and wearing a party dress.

It could be an ordinary death on a train:
a man calmly contemplating the fields and hills in snow
shuts his eyes, folds his hands in his lap,
and no longer sees what only a moment ago delighted him.

I'm trying to remember other possibilities, and so
here I am once again, disguised as myself
in a small, merry company, where after emptying my glass,
I fall on the floor laughing and pulling after me
the tablecloth with the vase full of roses.

My death, of course, would have an exalted meaning
in some mountain sanitorium for the insane
where, in beds with freshly changed sheets,
we complain to each other while expiring.

It could happen that I'll die in some way unlike the one I
    anticipate:
in the company of my wife and daughter,
surrounded by my books, while outdoors a neighbor is
    trying
to start a car that the night has surprised with snow.

from *Whores*

With me is a railroad man
in a railroad uniform,
with a railroad whistle and pocket watch,
and a railroad cap.

He talks about trains,
the express, the cannonball.
He remembers a girl
he left behind on the train.

Before he lies down
he turns off the lamp.
Outside, falling snowflakes
mingle with electric sparks.

Asleep he holds me
by my breasts,
still wearing his wool socks
with a toe sticking out of each one.

In the morning he runs
across the tracks.
He loses his cap.
He finds his cap.

With me is a man
who talks too much,
talks about everything,
so he sees nothing.

The washpan with red
and blue roses,
or the frog in the pan
with twelve baby frogs.

Sees neither my left
nor my right shoulder,
nor my cheeks caked
with thick powder.

Sees neither my thing,
nor his thing,
babbling so much he forgets
why he came.

I stuck a finger
under his tongue
and my finger stayed
in his mouth.

ॐ

With me is a young woman
who loves only women.
She smokes unfiltered cigarettes,
sways while she walks,

pays for my services
in foreign currency.
Her breasts are still
just two drops of honey.

she uses a whip,
sips ghastly concoctions.
We dream of each other,
exchange places.

When I wake, I see beside me,
my own funny childlike face
with buck teeth
and high cheek bones.

At night, a beard and a mustache
grow on her. In the morning,
she is again herself,
neither better nor worse than she is.

With me is a long-legged,
long-eared stallion.
His other horsy virtues
I won't even mention.

He bolted from under
his master's whip.
He's tired of high-class mares,
he wants only me.

He strokes me with his head
and his tufted mane.
He's happy when I ride him
naked, wearing only boots.

His eye is human
and so is his impatience
and his well-developed
sense of humor.

He eats blue-tinted sugar cubes
out of my hand.
In some respect, he's a man.
In others, just a horse.

With me is a grinning
skeleton,
when he walks, the bones
make a racket.

At times he loses
some small bone,
so we look for it
among the bedding.

Expertly, I fit
the missing bone between two others.
It's tiring work,
but it gives me pleasure.

At times, he tries to drink
from my glass.
The way the wine puddles on the floor
makes him truly miserable.

If he had any nerves,
he'd lose them in bed
having to listen
to the rattle of his bones.

✤

With me is the God
of all gods.
I have no other god
but him.

Without fuss
he kisses me everywhere:
on my head, on my forehead,
on my undone hair,

on my mouth while I speak,
in my armpits,
on my wet tits,
on my left and on my right knee,

inside my lungs, in my heart,
in my bowels,
in both kidneys,
and in my full and in my empty gut.

With great art he handles
the venerable tool.
God is truly within me,
or any other girl like me.

The rats

The granary is full of wheat, oats, and rye.
The millionaire and his wife ride in a glass coach.
The church door is open, the priest sits in a tavern.
Once more God makes make-believe crows suffer.

The fashionable woman paints her mouth in a cracked
    mirror.
Her shirt with a violet tail is turned inside out.
With all her memories, blood rushes into her cheek.
People drink out of saucers, eat with smaller and smaller
    knives and forks.

The rats are like smudges of Indian ink.
They watch out of floor cracks and other holes.
There's only one way to stroll in the meadow:
naked and barefoot, whimpering and with eyes lowered.

Happy is the watchmaker with the tiny parts of a clock.
Someone sits in shadow fingering objects of different value.
The rain touches the tent roof, searching for a hole.
We bump into many kinds of trees speaking incoherent
    sentences.

There's no way to move the lamps.
Everybody needs a precedent, some terrifying motive.
Rats swim upstream towed by a nylon thread.
They wear silk and are filled with almost human despair.

The bell tinkles in the working man's home.
The bread goes from one white hand to the other.
After a long, exhausting talk, friends recognize each other.
Cards are thrown on the table, children's laughter hovers
    like one of the household spirits.

The rat is different. He is master of the underworld:
junk dealer, lover of the lady with cotton in her ears.
He gnaws her small mouth, small tongue, small eyebrows,
the little foot in the little shoe, and the one with its shoe
    fallen off.

The millionaire and his wife rise out of the chimney.
One of them has crimson, and the other white wings.
Deep snow has fallen on both sides of the river.
The heavens have a cylindrical shape and can be enlarged,
    depending on need.

The keeper of the keys follows the mistress of the house.
Soon we'll see them in bed under a red crucifix.
The locks are unlocked, the wind nudges the small door
    open.
Disguised as a detective, the rat appears, followed
    by whispers and squeals.

Rats sit in chairs with high backs.
As always, military uniforms are fashionable this year.
The violinist leans on the cello-player and falls.
Those who have no business here belong with children
    and young women behind the door.

Rat the President and rat the First Secretary
play cards at the marble-topped table with iron legs.
The cane, the pipe and yesterday's newspapers float in the air
together with the comb, the letter-opener, and false teeth.

Gray-bristled, barely visible, a tail sticks out of the holy
    icon on the wall.
By the light of a petroleum lamp burning with a thin wick,
legs touch under the table,
the man's in heavy boots, the woman's in canvas shoes.

Mr and Mrs Ratso are snug in bed.
Their feet and tails show under the striped cover.
Other rats divert themselves reading literary compositions.
Outdoors, red-lettered banners lean against the house.

Her heart beats a hundred and twenty times per minute
when she sees the familiar snout and protruding teeth.
She takes off her dress. The rat trembles on her plump knee.
What is happiness without fear, at least to begin with?

Down the green staircase come informer rats
wearing informer uniforms studded with golden medals.
There are bigshots, super bigshots, kings and gaolers.
This city is busy finding accommodation for new arrivals
    disguised as rats.

The chief of the rats, cleanly-shaven and wearing civvies,
sits at an ornate writing-desk.
He makes decisions, signs proclamations, dreaming of being
wonderfully locked-up in a worm-eaten cellar with barrels
    of beer.

Watch out, the party is just starting! The future flies
toward us in the shape of the already symbolic flying rat.
We can't go outside, and we can't remain indoors.
The walls are weakening. Every house-beam is moving
   away from its neighbor. Even more terrifying images
   of rats, big and small, doing different things, lie ahead.

Four poems about wine

NOT AFTER BAUDELAIRE

I

Let's then, in an old-fashioned way, speak about wine,
stamping our feet, my dear, elbowing each other, flirting,
while swallows busy themselves in a hundred different
     ways between the house and the encircling sky,
while roses still bloom, somewhere by the open window,
     as they used to do in poems.

Here he is talking about wine, the lover of small dives
     and their wood stoves.
Here she is talking about it, too, the student of Aristotle
     chatting with a bare-chested wino.
And here is the tavern preacher with a small pulpit and a
     rooster and a sheep next to his pink knees.
And here is the traveler in the sled, big-assed, dim-eyed
     and with a ring on each finger.

Till yesterday you were at home, but now they look for
     you everywhere:
at the table, of course, and before the wonder-working
     mirror,
naked from waist down, stripping yourself every evening
     down to sweet suffering,
while make-believe gives way to reality: the whip, for
     instance, or the evil-minded hooks.

Here you are then in an odd place and in an odd
   predicament,
drunk with glory and wealth, drifting from room to room.
That's why you don't mind the girl passing in rapid
   images before you.
That's why you sit over a glass with a trace of lipstick on
   its rim.

2

For you who did not know me and are dying of envy
   because others did, this glass of wine!
For you young lady hanging your stockings and bra on the
   line, this glass of wine!
And for you Seneca, while I read your writings by the lamp
   with the bugs tapping on the windowpane.
And for you thief of another's man's verses, in whose
   poems some of these lines will be found . . .

It's easy to toast those one does not see or hear, and cannot
   touch.
Those, for instance, in a funeral procession who vanish
   behind the budding trees.
A drop of wine for the dead man fenced in by candles and
   paper ribbons with gold letters,
and for the dead woman in a starched shirt and a scarf tied
   around her chin.

A beautiful angel came, took the bottle out of our hands
    and sprinkled the rose bushes,
and the roses bloomed to the joy of the one who cherished
    them remembering other times and roses:
looks full of love, someone's wine-bloodied mouth,
and the guest in high boots in the snow who had a wooden
    toy in his hand.

As we climb the hill, they descend all muddied and laughing
    from too much wine,
as we bring our mother, they are already motherless, have
    red faces and hoarse voices,
as their dog pisses against a tree, ours still stands next to
    our polished shoes,
as we haul our heavy casket, they are already in bed vomiting
    the wine and the funeral cake into a bowl on the floor.

3

Not you glutton, but the one whose tongue and feet are
    entangled every afternoon.
Not you show-off, but the one in cahoots with the bottle in
    in which all sorts of clever ideas and quips lie stored.
Not you kid, who are like a peacock feather among chicken
    feathers, but the one who snores at the fat breast of an
    older woman, drunk from the first glass of wine.
And not you nobody, but the one who is *somebody* when
    he steps out of the tavern, flushed with wine, possessing
    everything he doesn't possess, naming things that cannot
    be named.

Not you royal wine, after the hunt in the lodge in the
  woods with dim mirrors and mutual suspicion,
nor you wine of the dying, being sipped by his bedside by
  those who feel themselves immortal while already in each
  window there's the red stain of the evening,
not you the idea of wine, as when we speak of light in the
  abstract, wine reduced to one meaning and use,
nor you wine whose tracks I try to hide in a poem about
  wine, myself silly with wine, holding by the waist the one
  who also talks about wine, sitting with me over morning
  mail and pastry.

The donkey knows nothing about wine as it climbs the hill
  carrying a woman naked and penniless, as in some rich
  man's reverie.
The politician in a crowd of like-minded followers, drunk
  with wine without knowing anything about wine,
  daydreams about farms and factories, rose-gardens in
  every schoolyard.
The wine is kind to the one who finds himself in an
  imaginary snowstorm rushing to visit friends only to
  be met by a landlady and her daughter who has a breast
  peeking out of her blouse like one more face,
and is unkind to the schoolgirl who runs around speaking
  Latin better than her mother tongue in the accent of
  some new suburb. With each sip she rises from the
  ground by a couple of inches together with the equally
  levitating glasses.

Good wine can be found, too, where writers and their pets
    feast each other with ink.
The rural mail arrives in the evening bringing some
    nonsense written over wine and the lady of the house in
    bed.
The clerks sweep the snow so they can get to their desks
    and the sheets of paper crumpled in their wastebaskets,
but that's not my problem. I stare at what's in front of me:
    the bread and the wine.

4

To the face in the bright mirror, who is neither you nor I,
    but a sweet young Miss, a glass of wine is welcome.
You sunbathe first the left and then the right shoulder, take
    off your bra and reveal a sight worthy of the highest
    praise.
The table, the bed and the wine before your richly made-up
    face have turned green from the overhanging leaves.
One can hear green music played on green instruments by
    good-for-nothings of both sexes.

We'll fly from place to place in silk suits and silk dresses,
while at the table the polite couple sit, her breasts visible
    like two brown eyes through the transparent fabric.
We'll land on the meadow before the cold hits us in the
    face or nails us to some invisible god's trees and crosses,
while in the house two guests sit blinded by wine which has
    dripped on the bed covers and the stockings stuffed into
    nicely polished shoes.

We'll fly with books under arms, like a husband and wife
   ideally matched to the music of whips swishing,
over the stone city with a drop of blood in each one of its
   windows, with just one idea in our heads, to be flying.
The mocking won't reach us, nor the hoot of the owl, nor
   the constant cracking of trees,
only the sound of this sentence will, as it holds on to
   another sentence, and then still another, whose meaning
   depends on the season.

Now it's time for a glass of wine and a small cake
   accompanied by a cat meowing and the swaying of the
   table –
Aristotle's wine fortified by never-ending dispute between
   water, wheat and bed.
I'm sitting alone over a glass, untouched by the jibes of my
   neighbors and poets in violet-colored uniforms.
Light shines on my crimson fingers as they hold the crimson
   glass and on the invisible face of the one I'll mention
   some other time, swaying as I rise, drunk, of course, with
   some other wine and light.